Peter Garball
aug 04

Yet Another Home

Yet Another Home

POEMS

Peter Jailall

NATURAL HERITAGE/NATURAL HISTORY INC.

Copyright © 1997 by Peter Jailall

All rights reserved. No portion of this book, with the exception of brief extracts for the purpose of literary or scholarly review, may be reproduced in any form without the permission of the publisher.

Published by Natural Heritage/Natural History Inc.
P.O. Box 95, Station O, Toronto, Ontario M4A 2M8

First Edition

Canadian Cataloguing in Publication Data

Jailall, Peter
  Yet another home

Poems.
ISBN 1-896219-14-4

I. Title

PS8569. A414Y48 1996   C811'.54   C96-931560-0
PR9199. 3.J34Y48 1996

Design by Norton Hamil Design
Cover illustration by Blanche Hamil

Natural Heritage/Natural History Inc. acknowledges the support received for its publishing program from the Canada Council Block Grant Program. We also acknowledge with gratitude the assistance of the Association for the Export of Canadian Books, Ottawa, and the Office of the Ontario Arts Council, Toronto.

PRINTED IN CANADA BY MOTHERSILL PRINTING

Dedicated to Sabi, Dave and Nari.

Foreword

I first met Peter Jailall through his writing. Peter consistently wrote articles for *The Beacon*, The Educators' Association newspaper for the Peel Board of Education and I was one of hundreds of readers who would often be caught up with Peter's insights, views and arguments about issues in education. Then, about a decade ago, Peter and I became neighbours on the second floor of Queenston Drive Public School and we would share conversations on many an afternoon. Ideas were always percolating in Peter's head and seldom would he hesitate to share views on cultural or political topics during our little chats.

A couple of years ago with the publication of his first poetry collection *This Healing Place and Other Poems* I recognized that Peter's perceptions were not resting quietly in his head. Through words, Peter is able to weave a tapestry of images from immigrant, racial and human experiences. Recently, I came upon this comment from May Hill Arbuthnot who said that "like music, poetry comes with healing in its wings; it carries its own therapy" and I am confident that poetic word arrangements give Peter healing of spirit and wings to fly.

In this new anthology, Peter once again draws on his heritage from the Caribbean and from his life as a Canadian citizen, inviting readers to contemplate social justice and challenging them to journey into their own visions of belonging. These poems by appealing both to thought and feeling, convey the power to call up sharp sensory images in the reader and evoke rich emotional responses. The poems both illuminate and clarify. Peter's poetry deepens ordinary experience and helps us see a little differently, whether describing the immigrant experience in *Yet Another Home*, is a "disoriented wanderer/ without stick or rudder, whether paying tribute to the

Foreword

people in his life as he does in *My Grandfather* ("My grandfather is wise/He tells no lies," or expressing a quiet rage as he does in *Feeling Alone* ("I hurt deep inside/From the collective force/Of the power drill? that tears through my heart.").

In one poem, Peter himself claims that poets "cast words helping others live their lives." Thank you, Peter, for your spirit, your soul and for your words that help us live our lives. Here in this book you have found "Yet Another Home."

You are a poet.

Larry Swartz–educator, author

Acknowledgments

Larry Swartz, Jim Giles, Judaman Seecomar and Sabi Jailall

Contents

Foreword ix

Acknowledgments xi

Introduction 3

Poets 5

X People 6

The Old Country 7

The Rice Christian Prayer 8

I Remember 10

Walking in Winter 12

Freeze 14

MacDonald in Toronto 15

On Georgian Bay 16

Christmas 17

When Nazmoon Died 18

The Return of the Expatriate 19

Village Talk 20

Estate Talk 21

Caribbean Man Talk 22

Canada Wear 23

June 29th 24

For Those of Us Who Wear Red 25

Yet Another Home 27

The Best Canadian Tool 29

Contents

Telegram from Gold Digging   *30*

Our Manifest Destiny   *31*

Paddling to Pakouri   *32*

Feeling Alone   *33*

My Dog Ricey   *34*

1962   *35*

Shattered Dream   *36*

When Death Comes   *38*

Fear   *40*

Simple Things   *42*

A Teacher's Nightmare   *43*

Letter to Joyce T.   *44*

Mississauga Field Mouse   *45*

For the Young

Hallowe'en Night   *49*

Daddy Please Recycle   *51*

Falling Leaves   *52*

A Bad Hair Day   *53*

In the Jungle   *54*

Latch Key Kid   *55*

My Country   *56*

My Grandfather   *57*

Yet Another Home

Introduction

Canadians come from all corners of the globe—some as refugees fleeing persecution, even death. Others have come earlier crossing dangerous waters to join the First Nation peoples in search of a better life for themselves and their children.

Canada is a haven for many people who have come from remote corners of the globe.

Many Guyanese have also chosen to make Canada their home, settling here in large numbers during the seventies and mid-eighties. In my first book *This Healing Place and Other Poems,* I addressed the challenges Guyanese faced as a new immigrant group, how they settled and adjusted to a harsh climate and a new landscape, their encounter with racism and their abandonment of their homeland to start life anew in Canada.

In this my second book *Yet Another Home,* my poems focus on Guyanese-Canadians, no longer a new immigrant group, but a cultural group that has integrated into the Canadian mainstream.

Poems in this second book address the settlement of our seniors and their grandchildren in their new Canadian home. For the seniors and for the wider Canadian and Caribbean audience, I re-entered the Guyanese culture back home to remind myself and my readers and listeners of both our new and old homes.

The section, For The Young, is suitable for all young Canadians who enjoy listening and reading poetry that talks about the emergence of a Canadian culture that always keeps renewing itself.

Peter Jailall

Poets

Like blacksmiths banging iron
To smooth out rough edges

Like farmers scattering seeds
To germinate in spring

Like the village preacher's call
Exhorting
Challenging
Provoking
Disturbing
We cast words
Helping others live their lives.

X People

Across blackwaters
My people came searching
Strangers in strange clothing
Tied in one big knot
Looking for a new home
Sweating beads
Sheltering from heavy white rain
Gargling salt water
To cure sore throats
Dreaming of light work
And quick money
Bending double
Coughing and working
In an open furnace
Learning a new language
And making their mark
On the bottom line.

The Old Country

When I revisit the old country
I run for shelter
Hiding from a hostile sun
That melts the sole
of my cowskin sandals
And freezes my spine
From the wetness of my shirt
My ancestral home is a prison
Rough iron bars painted in white
Stick out like a million crosses
In a vast decorated cemetery
Across the land
Fluorescent lights keep watch
So I can steal some sleep
And when the blackouts come
The chilling silence is broken
Only by a human cough
Or a drunkman's song
I await the morning light
When fear and darkness
Are driven out
And life returns anew
In the old country.

The Rice Christians' Prayer

One by one
The rice Christians gathered
On top of canal dam
For their regular open air
Loud and clear
They sang their opening prayer:
"When we all get to heaven
What a day of rejoicing
that will be.
When we all see Jesus
We will sing and shout
for victory."

The angry Hindu elders heard
The rice Christians' victory song
Confronted the converts
As they sang
Gave Pal and Silas
Some prapa licks
With their big fat ackya sticks
They muttered under their fiery breath:
"Abe gu mash a yu skin tenight
Beat out de whiteman religion
And nack some sense in a yu hed
A yu gan maad or wha?
How can Ram and Krishna tun
Pal an Silas?
Can sheep tun goat?
A yu wan tun blackman, nuh?"

"They knocked their Bibles to the ground
And gave them a good licking
But the stubborn rice Christians stood unmoved
Like a giant coconut tree

The Rice Christians' Prayer

> Swaying by the water
> And with heads thrown back
> And empty hands outstretched
> They gazed to the heavens above:
> "We gladly suffer as martyrs
> For thee O lord"
>
> "And there will be no sorrow there
> In my Father's House
> In my Father's House
> In my Father's House
> There will be no sorrow there
> In my Father's House
> There will be joy, joy, joy"

I Remember

I remember
The little red top house
With its porch jutting out
And a rotten black post
At the end of a narrow platform

I remember
The house where I was born
We huddled together
On grandma's fence
Sitting on that narrow platform
Sucking red crushed ice
On hot days
And chewing brown sugar cane
On cool nights
Swatting sandflies
With our sticky hands

I remember
Kala's cake shop
Where we bought rock buns
And red stretcher sweetie

I remember highbridge
From where we plunged
Into the foaming river

I remember Parson yard
With the giant palm trees swaying
We shared the shade
With a herd of cows
After a vigorous cricket game

I Remember

I remember Parson iron gate
Where we took turns swinging
And the pebbled entrance
Where we bounced marbles for buttons
Swapping many prized multicoloured buttons
When our marbles kissed

I remember the old English coins
That we found in Parson yard
Now I have forgotten–
How those old coins and buttons looked
For they are all buried deep
Under Parson yard, asleep.

Walking in Winter

    Crunch!   Crunch!
                                Crunch!
It begins a a carefree,
                meditative journey
                          through…
the crunching snow

                But soon
                          the crunch crunch

disappears

And I become oblivious of everything
                              below.

As in a trance
            my senses take in
the lioness of winter
            I close my eyes
                      But
I still see a cold blackbird
            balancing
      swaying on a frozen wire

      Her hungry eyes searching
                            over
        the white wilderness

Suddenly, she dashes away with a great
              gust of wind

Walking in Winter

    I see avalanches
              gliding
                      slowly
                              down
                                        roof tops

Then swiftly toppling over

I draw pictures in my mind
        Red apples on white boughs
                Bees in tropical trees
                        sucking nectar

        Brown ice-cream cones
        A dozen flavours pressed down
        On a sunny beach

Bodies dusted in yellow sand

CRUNCH! CRUNCH! CRUNCH!

I'm awakened by a sharp curry smell
        It's winter in Canada.

Freeze

In front of Acme Photo studio
The beggar woman sits, half-naked
Head bent, close to her knees
Her withered hands outstretched–
A perfect pose
She wiggles her toes
To drive the flies away
Her toenails near decay
I have seen her before
In her younger days–
Energetic, strong-willed, happy and proud
Singing hymns, scrubbing washboards
To send her children clean to school
She lived dignified, never whining
Now, no one cares about her
Her burning hunger
Her dirty feet, her nakedness
She's no stranger
Someone's mother, our mother
Sitting in front of Acme Studio
Drying out like a wall flower.

MacDonald in Toronto

Dressed in an old red plaid shirt
His possessions in a Glad garbage bag
MacDonald sits alone
On a park bench in Toronto
Watching different people as they go.

From the park bench
He staggers awkwardly on the grass
Outside Queen's Park
Feeding pigeons
Before it gets too dark.

Later at night
He drifts on the street
Rolls out his bed to sleep
Opens his bottle for a nightcap
Officers disturb him with a gentle tap.

MacDonald on the park bench in Toronto
There's no other place for him to go.

On Georgian Bay

Alone,
On the choppy waters
On Georgian Bay
Looking at
White boats dancing
Against the giant birch
Her apex pinpointing
The vertex of the V
Intersecting the gaggle of Canada geese
Gliding purposefully through the clear blue sky

Alone,
On the choppy waters
On Georgian Bay
I now know that
I'm an important species
Privileged to enjoy God's beauty.

Christmas

> Christmas comes every year
> And each person must have a share
> Even the prisoner in the jail
> Drinking sour ginger ale.

When Nazmoon Died

They came for her
On that purple morning
Like hissing snakes
Set free from their blackpits

They crawled on naked bellies
Among the tall blacksage bush
Charged with rage and hate

Her husband sprang
Out the back window
Like a frightened cat
With one child slung on his back
Leaving Nazmoon alone
Helpless
With the unborn
Struggling
To break the wall of the womb;
Paralyzed
She begged quietly: "Look at my condition
Oh! Please spare my life
For the sake of the baby inside."

But the man fired one deadly shot
Straight to her womb
Felling mother and child on the spot

That purple morning when Nazmoon died
The baby inside never cried.

The Return of the Expatriate

Suddenly, the 747 thunders and claps
Above the musical noise of the jungle
It descends on the boiling runway
Full speed ahead
Slows down, then turns to the WELCOME sign
The expatriate disembarks
Armed with video camera, glittering watch
Bottles of Western water
And chocolate bars
He pops pink bubble gum
As he sizes up the crowd
His fat wallet bulging
With foreign currency
All eyes follow him
Walking tall among the crowd
A sea of family members quickly
Encircle him
Touching,
    Touching…
        Touching his
            foreign technology.

Village Talk

Eh! Eh!
Luk how al dem gal
A walk a dam now-a-daze
Wid dem big, big bellie
Wen me bin a get me Kennet
Me bin ga fu haal meself in de yaad
Til dem ole people pass
Becaze–dem sey
me bin bruk stick ah me aze
An me ga fu tek de shame
But now-a-daze
de shame
A na fu mek de picknee
But a fu play
Buk and key
Fu know
A who a de dadee

Estate Talk

Auntie Finey
Standing by de Pailin
Engaging in discourse:
    "A wen you cum, bet?"
    "Me cum yestiday auntie"
    "A how you do na bet?"
    "Me deh auntie"
    "How you du?"

"Wa me gu tell you, me picknee
Pain a kill me
Ya walk al ova me baady"
    "Ah how uncle do, Auntie?"

"Beti, da man a ge me too much worries
As soon as e get e money
E gaan a rum shap
Night an day ya dhakolay daru
Da man da
Na kay if
Good Friday faal
Pan a Sateday."

Caribbean Man Talk

BLACKman	WHITEman
COOLIEman	BUCKman
PUTAGEEman	CHINEEman
DOUGLAman	REDman
BROTHERman	ANTIman
BOSSman	BUSINESSman
CHANNAman	MILKman
POSTman	POLICEman
OILman	WOODman
OBEAHman	RASTAman

BADman	feared man
BADwoman	prostitute

Canada Wear

No Jack! not me
Wearing a shirtjac
Not here in Canada
I'm no hairdresser
I come to this country
To improve meself
To wear three-piece and wristwatch
Look chap!
I used to ride jackass
Now me a ride iyan hass

June 29th

Sometimes, happy times
Sometimes, sad times
But always pressing on
Living together nicely
Travelling daily
Sipping hot coffee
When winter's cold
And growing old
We're seldom lonely
In each other's company.

For Those of Us Who Wear Red

Stop! British soldier, stop!
Halt! You and your mate
Look before you enter the estate
Stop! Can't you see?
Red means danger
So don't rush in to plunder
Ripping our Jhandi flags asunder
To stop Communism in Guyana.

Stop! City bureaucrat, stop!
Red means anger
We are always willing to suffer
Dressed up in our red Sunday best
To attend Congress
Or hustling to Gem cinema
For our Saturday afternoon adventure.

Stop! Professor, stop!
Red means sacrifice
Especially in June
Our sacred month of Red
When our martyrs' blood was shed
Come write about us
Write about how we cut up ourselves
Like swampfield fish
With our sharp cutlish

Stop! Philosopher, Stop!
Red means devotion
We sprinkle abeer
Rub sindoor
Draw lifelines
Knotting Rakhi red thread–
Bonds that bind us
To struggle for our daily bread

For Those of Us Who Wear Red

        Stop! Mighty army, stop!
        Red means danger
        So look before you enter
        Think before you dig your heavy boots
        Into our tender ratoon shoots.

Yet Another Home

My father
Homeless since indentureship
A disoriented wanderer
Without stick or rudder
Set adrift
From a cloudless tropical sky
Dropped near a frozen lake
Without friends
Land or seeds.
Cows or beads.

Yesterday,
He walked proud
Looking over ricefield lands
Feeling settled
Hands gripped tight
Behind his back
Whistling with canaries

Today,
He stumbles along
An alien
In his sterilized seniors' home
Watching sheepishly
White-haired women
Giggling and poking coloured balls
Across artificial green fields
He smiles as he watches them
Polishing the tip of their stick
He carried a stick like that once
To disembark from the ship
To steer tired oxen
And to measure distances
Between banana trees.

Yet Another Home

Now,
During his cold Canadian days
He hides inside
Circles a peephole
With the tip of his ancient nose
On the frosty window pane
His eyes following
A solitary snow-covered milk truck
Ploughing through the virgin snow
Delivering homogenized milk
Pumped out of helpless holsteins

My father gets tired easily
Reads a book about Jim Jones
And his People's Temple
Nods,
Slowly falls asleep
Dreaming
Of yet another far-away home.

The Best Canadian Tool

In the cold, cold
Cold Canadian winter
When sheets of ice
Glaze windshields
So much depends
Upon
A small ice scraper
Abandoned in the car trunk
Beneath the ice cooler
In the hot, hot
Hot Canadian summer.

Telegram From Gold Digging

"Hello! Hello!

>Thundered Brother Sovereign's voice through the jungle.

"Over! Over!"

>The village postmaster answered.

"This is Ocean Shark, P.M"

"Yes Sir!

"Can you write good English?"

>He asked

"I can write the Queen's English"

>The P.M. replied.

"Well, Exercise your English,"

>Commanded Brother Sovereign

"Write!-"

>OCEAN SHARK TO ANGEL BABY
>
>"Coming home soon
>Prepare fish broth
>If you don't have money, borrow!
>Gold in abundance."

Our Manifest Destiny

        O Canada
        Decorated lover
        In Red and White
        Traipsing across the globe
        Enticing young talent
        Luring them out
        Of their humble homestead
        Making new Canadians
        Eager builder
        Believer in the dream
        Ending up
        Homeless
        Motherless
        Helpless
        Stuck!
        O Canada!

Paddling to Pakouri

The engine beats, sputters
Leaving a smoky trail
Chasing living things away
From this open, natural zoo
Propelling us to Pakouri
Along the winding Mahaicony
To meet the First Nation
We call Amerindian
Living on St. Francis Mission

They welcome us
Feed us local fruits
Fresh deer meat
Washed down with water
From the creek.

They teach us
The ways of the forest
About herbal medicine
The age of trees and killer bees
Animal tracks and tropical fish
They are real ecologists

They paddle silently
In their dug out canoes
Moving timelessly
On their endless journey.

Feeling Alone

I hurt deep inside
From the collective force
Of the power drill
That rips through my heart
For the good I try to do
No medicine can cure the betrayed
I scrub the hurt
With fake smiles
Living under the weight
Of heavy melancholy
Working hard to prove myself
Knowing my best will not be enough
Finding no one to turn to
When friends are gone
And the exterminator takes over.

My Dog Ricey

for Ernie K.

Long ago in the Land of Plenty
Along the shores of Lake Erie
Dogs lived in luxury
In a big white house
Even better than dem dogs
Across the lake

Today, in the Land of Plenty
Dogs still live in luxury
Visit doctors, receive prescriptions
And are admitted to their own hospitals
They are kissed and loved
Coaxed and tucked in quilted beds
Dressed up in tartan coats
Act in movies
Driven in expensive cars
Bark in their own food aisle
Especially when they see
Doctor Ballard's finest choices
They have impressive names
Like the British bulldogs of old–
Clifford, Drake, Rover and Dover

In the Land of Scarcity
Lives my poor Ricey
Hungry belly
Mangy
Eyes watery
Sits under the bottom house
Alone
Chewing on a dry catfish bone

1962

Run! Run! Run!
Blackman a cum

Run! Run! Run!
Coolie a cum

Run! Run! Run!
Run out de tung
Befoe de tung bun down

Run! Run! Run!
Run out de estate
Befoe e get too late

Run! Run! Run!
Blackman a fight
Coolie a fight
Al a dem a lick down
Al a dem a shoot down
Al a dem a bun down

Run! Run! Run!
Steamship a cum

Run! Run! Run!
Blackman a run
Coolie a run
Al a dem a run

Hide! Hide! Hide!
Blackman a hide
Coolie a hide
Al a dem a hide
When backra put de curfew
Pan dem backside.

Shattered Dream

Along Anandale's narrow road
Just near market square
Animals, metal and people clash:
Ambling cows, canting ducks
Frisky goats, nervous sheep
Sluggish pigs, galloping horses
Running before loaded sand trucks
Flying Minibuses
Rattling old Morris-Oxfords
Staggering drunkards
Children bent with water buckets
Women steadying ration baskets

Along Anandale's narrow road
Just near market square
The truckman swerved his heavy truck
To save the confused drunk
Killed the young woman instantly
Dashed her to the ground
Crushed her head
White grey matter oozed out
Like mayonnaise from a water spout
A man offered his white shirt
To cover her head
For human dignity
Her hand sticking out
To wave the world goodbye
An elderly woman whispered:
"Ou Bhagwan,
She was so young and nice
Working to help her widowed mother
Waiting for an outside boy
For marriage
To take her to America for good."

Shattered Dream

> O death, you brute!
> You cheat!
> You beat him to it
> On Anandale's narrow road.

When Death Comes

Death must not catch me sleeping
One of these days, I tell you
One of these good days
I'm going to drive to the airport
I'm making no sport
I'm going to park
Beside the other abandoned cars
Buy a one-way ticket
And I'll leave this crazy place for good
I'll turn me back
And never come back
Here, I live a big fat lie
I want to experience the good life
Before I die.
I want to escape
To this beautiful island
Near Cinderella county
To wake up in the morning
By the gentle cooing of doves
And the peaceful rippling of the waves
I want to hear the pebbles roll on the beach
To grow callaloo and tomatoes
Without acid rain
Rock in my Amerindian hammock
With a wooden pipe clenched
Between me teeth
I want to relax
Stop this running
And racing along the 401.
I want to live in peace
Near God.
And when I die
I want the local carpenters
To make me a wooden box

When Death Comes

With pure Guyana wood
I want them to line it
With a clean, white chadhar
And make me look nice
With fresh red hibiscus
Smiling around me
I want the village people
To sing out loud
And to knock the gong
To keep me company
As they carry me
On that lonely journey
To the burial ground
I want them to throw dutty on me
As they chant, "Om Shanti, Shanti!"

Fear

After some heavy bargaining
For a reasonable fare–
A fare higher than the big ferry
For half an hour's ride
Instead of a three hour cruise
The teenage captain herd us down
Into the dungeon
Under Parika stelling
Holds my nervous hand
So I can board
The stationary speed boat
Tied to a post
With a frayed piece of rope
I leap in
Balancing myself
And the other eighteen souls on board
Given pieces of yellow plastic
To cover ourselves
From head to toe
To keep the splashing water out.

The teenage captain starts the engine
And the speed boat zooms
Jumping over the high waves

I feel sick to my stomach
I close my eyes
I can hear the loud noise
From the engine
And the loud clapping
Of the waves against the bow
In this watery wilderness
The passengers talk with their eyes

Fear

I peep through the hole
Of my plastic covering
All I can see is
Water, water everywhere

I bend double
I close my eyes
I press my ears
I recite the poem
The Rime of the Ancient Mariner
I recite the Lord's Prayer
I think of my children, my will
I ask God to save my life
And I'll serve him forever
I raise my head for some air
The speed boat is travelling near an island
My heart beat slows down
If we sink, I will be able to swim
The child sitting beside me smiles
The teenage captain disengages the engine
I step on land, vowing
Never to ride the speed boat again
In the mighty Essequibo River.

Simple Things

The candle fly lights up my path
Through the pitch dark night

The kiskadee awakes me
With its melody rich and sweet

The bull frog calls for rain
When the earth is dry

The crow circles overhead
To warn about the dead

Why must these simple creatures disappear?

A Teacher's Nightmare

> Just half asleep
> Tossing and turning
> Coaxing and caressing
> My poor pillow
> For comfort, security, warmth
> Squinting low beams
> Into the ceiling
> Coloured beads streaming across
> Taking my class attendance twice
> Top to bottom
> Bottom to top
> Thinking of tomorrow
> The alarm goes off
> I hope morning never comes.

Letter to Joyce T.

I miss you.
Everytime I go home
Wata cum to me eye
I remember you telling me
How tick you an you
East Indian friend Lila
Used to be
How you suck de same sweetie
How you meet pan High Street
Hug up an cry in 1962
Because you used to live good.
Well, tings still baad.
Daag eat daag
Money nuff nuff
Food dear, dear
People scare scare
Friken a kick chuch a nite
Too much cussing
Little respects
School like ded house
Picknie na a laan
Palitics caan full bellie
Who go way
Kaak duck
Call you expatriate
Pampaset, suspect
You cum back fuh wuk, nuh?
Stay in England, cool breeze!

Mississauga Field Mouse

On a dry summer's day
A lonely field mouse came out to play
Tumbling a single bale of hay
Hiding it under
The rose bush tree
When the sputtering lawn mower approached
He stood on his small hind legs
Remembering the great excavation
That chased his family away
The monster machine levelled
Everything in sight
Digging up trees
Driving away bees
Covering the children's hockey pond
Where the tiny fish egg
Floated in spring
The lonely field mouse hid
In the bale of hay
Under the rosebush tree
Until the lawnmower turned away
Unnoticed, he made his escape
Into the open garage
Slipped under a pile of cartoon boxes
Where he lived through the summer
Into the winter
Feeding on garbage crumbs
One winter's night, the homeowner spied him
Running from under
The warm car engine
Determined to sanitize his garage
He bought a box of green cross
Made four neat piles
In the corners of the field mouse's abode
Determined to exterminate him–
Forever.

For the Young

Halloween Night

Halloween night
Is the darkest night
When witches race in flight
Children run
Out and about
Filling the air
With a joyful shout:
    "Trick or treat
    We are neat
    Give us something good to eat"

Halloween night
Is the darkest night
When goblins prance and fight
Children run
Out and about
Filling their bags
With delicious treats:
    "Apples, Smarties, Nuts and Chips
    We will crunch
    And lick our lips"

Halloween night
Is the darkest night
When bats use their radar sight
Children run
Out and about
Filling their stomachs
With sugary stuff:
    "Candies, Toffees, Chocolates, Gum
    We will chew
    Yum! Yum! Yum!

Halloween Night

>Halloween night
>Is the darkest night
>When cats' eyes are fiery bright
>Children run
>Out and about
>Filling their neighbourhood
>With garbage delight:
>>"Candy wrappers, Apple core
>>Torn costumes
>>And much, much more."

Daddy Please Recycle

Please, my daddy
Recycle that
Don't throw that out
In the garbage–
That goes in the recycle box
We must save Mother Earth you know
Already, the fish are dying
The trees are crying
Their leaves are suffocating
Drooping from the cars and factory smoke
Daddy, this is no joke
For there's no more joy
To the fishes
Even in the deep blue sea
And certainly no joy left
For you or for me.

Falling Leaves

>Leaves fall on the ground
>Telling us Autumn's just around
>I rake the fallen leaves
>Watchful of stinging bees
>Pile the leaves in one big heap
>Just before I make a leap
>Now, it's late to fool around
>A green garbage bag must be found
>To carry the leaves to the garden plot
>I'll make a compost in my spot.

A Bad Hair Day

I hate
To go to school
On Monday morning
After I had a mushroom cut
Because I feel ugly
And stupid

I hate
When the teacher says,
"Take that hat off!"

I wish
I could keep it on
To hide my head today

But I'll have to wait
Like Sampson between the posts
Until my hair grows back again.

In the Jungle

Up a high, high mountain
The Demerara River flows
And the Camoudi grows
Camouflages and hides

In the thick, thick jungle
Far above the high, high mountain
Deep into the clear, blue sky
The chicken hawk soars
Surveys and searches

In the thick, thick jungle
Among the purple heart trees
The star apple shivers
The white faced monkey feeds
Teases and chases

In the thick, thick jungle
Under the tall green trees
On the banks of the swift Demerara
The lazy alligator blinks
When the small mosquito bites.

Latch Key Kid

Every morning
At 8 o'clock
When I get dressed for school
No one's there to see
But I always heed my mother's plea:
"Don't forget!" she will say
"Remember to take your key today."

I hate to carry a key
Around my neck all day
Especially when I'm out to play.

Occasionally
I'll check to see
If I have lost my key

Then I'll check again at four
Before I enter my front door
Slowly, slowly
I'll turn my key
Then I'll enter fearfully.

My Country

I want to go back
To my country
Because I don't like the long winter
And the heavy clothes make me hot

I want to go back
To my country
Because I don't like the noise
And the furnace wakes me up

I want to go back
To my country
Because I don't see my mom
She goes to work before I'm up

I want to go back
To my country
Because I have no friends
And I'm lonely here

I want to go back
To my country
But who will take me?
So I'll wait until I am big enough to go.

Back to my country.

My Grandfather

My grandfather does not have a clock
He does not even wear a watch
He watches time on T.V.
Until he falls asleep
He sings old favourite songs to me
Especially when I'm lonely.

My grandfather does not have a cane
Occasionally, he bends over in pain
I comb his grey hair
He combs my black hair
Especially when mine gets tangled.

My grandfather is kind
He gives me sweetie and money
He's my sweet sugar daddy.

My grandfather is wise
He tells no lies
He only tells me stories
Of life, long, long ago.

A NOTE ABOUT THE AUTHOR

Peter Jailall, born in 1944 in Guyana, then known as British Guiana, attended the Government Training College for Teachers. Following graduation, he taught at Enmore School for five years.

In 1970, Peter came to Canada where he attended York University and the University of Toronto. A member of the Racial Minority Writer's Collective, Peter Jailall is a full member of The Canadian League of Poets. He has read his poetry to children, parents and teachers across Canada, in the Caribbean and in London, England. An avid supporter of human rights and social justice, Peter expresses his compassion and passion for human values through poetry.

Today, Peter teaches with the Peel Board of Education in Mississauga, where he lives with his wife Sabi, and their two sons, Dave and Nari. He enjoys gardening, fishing and cricket.

BOOKS OF POETRY FROM NATURAL HERITAGE

This Healing Place and Other Poems
Peter Jailall

"In this anthology, Peter Jailall draws experiences from his Caribbean heritage and from his Toronto life to produce poetry that challenges us to listen and to look again. There are no subdued voices here; only ones loaded with passion, candor and lively speech rhythms."–Bob Barton

ISBN 0-920474-84-5/96 pages/6˝x9˝/$9.95 SC

The Mulch Pile and Other Poems
Robert W. Nero
Drawings by James A. Carson

Ornithologist, ecologist, naturalist and poet, Dr. Robert Nero of Winnipeg is the acknowledged North American authority on the Great Gray Owl. Among a lengthy and impressive list of honours and awards, Nero was the first recipient of the Ernest Thompson Seton Award, presented by the Manitoba Naturalists Society in 1981.

ISBN 0-920474-83-7/96 pages/6˝x9˝/10 original line drawings/$9.95 SC

Woman by the Shore and Other Poems: A Tribute to Louise de Kiriline Lawrence
Robert W. Nero

Original line drawings by James A. Carson. Dr. Robert Nero demonstrates his admiration and affection for this remarkable woman through his environmentally sensitive and insightful poetry.

ISBN 0-920474-59-4/52 pages/6˝x9˝/$9.95 SC

Books of Poetry from Natural Heritage

The Salamander's Laughter and Other Poems
Anne Corkett
Drawings by Sylvia Hahn

"*The Salamander's Laughter and Other Poems* offers very good poems, small, lovely artifacts—flints chipped with a consummate patience and skill from the dense midden of ancient verse. ...stimulating and pertinent models for developing young tastes for both reading and writing poetry. Every detail, from page layout to type selection and paper choice contributes to the impression of fine quality. Each poem is faced with an illustration, in black and white."—Canadian Children's Literature Review

ISBN 0-920474-35-7/62 pages/5½"x8½"/$8.95 SC